WOK

Dishes from China, Japan, and Southeast Asia

WOK

Dishes from China, Japan,
and Southeast Asia

Elsa Petersen-Schepelern

photography by **Jeremy Hopley**

RYLAND
PETERS
& SMALL

LONDON NEW YORK

First published in the United States in 1998
This edition published 2002
by Ryland Peters & Small, Inc.
519 Broadway, 5th Floor
New York, NY 10012
www.rylandpeters.com

10 9 8 7 6 5 4 3 2 1

Library of Congress Cataloging-in-Publication Data
is available on request

ISBN 1 84172 360 6

Printed and bound in China

Designers Penny Stock, Sailesh Patel
Editor Maddalena Bastianelli
Production Meryl Silbert
Art Director Gabriella le Grazie
Publishing Director Alison Starling

Food Stylist Annie Nichols
Stylist Wei Tang

Acknowledgments
My thanks to my nephew Luc Votan for his expert advice on Vietnamese
dishes, my sister Kirsten, Peter Bray, Clare Ferguson, Susan, and Tim—and to
Faziah Fatah who asked me to do this book.
Thanks also to Habitat UK, who were so generous in lending us woks and
other props for photography.

Notes
All spoon measurements are level unless otherwise noted.
Speciality Asian ingredients are available in large supermarkets, Thai, Chinese,
Japanese, and Vietnamese stores.

contents

wok lore

The wok is one of the world's most versatile pieces of cooking equipment, used to stir-fry, deep-fry, steam, braise, or smoke foods. The traditional wok (**1**) is made of carbon steel and must be seasoned before use. Modern variations on this simple utensil are available, including nonstick surfaces (**2**), flat bases for use on electric stoves (**3**), and even plug-in electric woks.

The traditional wok includes two looped handles (**4**), which should be used with a cloth or oven glove to protect your hands from the heat. Others have a long wooden handle (**5**) or a handle plus a loop (**6**).

To season and clean a carbon steel wok

Scrub well with abrasive cleaner to remove machine oil used in manufacture. Rinse and dry. Heat 2 tablespoons vegetable oil in the wok, wipe it all over, and keep hot for 20 minutes. Pour out the oil and wipe the wok with paper towels until the paper is clean. The wok should never be washed in soap again, but only wiped clean with paper towels when still warm, or rinsed with water only, then dried carefully. Any persistent dirt can be scrubbed off with salt and/or a wok brush (**9**). Store the wok upside down to avoid rust.

Wok equipment

Special wok equipment includes a clip-on side rack (**7**) for draining food, as well as a round smoking rack (**8**) and a wok cleaning brush (**9**). Wok stands should be made of wire if using on gas; others are metal with side holes.

Other equipment includes a long-handled spoon, known as a charn, used for stir-frying (**10**), perforated and wire spoons for deep-frying (**11**), multitiered bamboo steamers (**12**), long-handled ladles (**13**), and long cooking chopsticks (**14**). A lid (**15**) is useful, especially for smoking and braising.

15

vietnamese
watercress soup

In Vietnam, this simple traditional soup is made with chrysanthemum leaves, and if you have access to a good Asian market, you can try it made in the classic way. Watercress, however, with its peppery flavor and the texture contrast between soft leaves and crunchy stems, is a good substitute. Add it at the very end, because it wilts very fast. If fish sauce is hard to find, use extra salt instead.

Heat the oil in a wok, add the shrimp shells, ginger, garlic, and lemongrass and stir-fry until the shells change color. Keep stir-frying for a few minutes to extract some of the flavor and color. Transfer to the bowl of fish stock.

Add the scallions to the wok and stir-fry for 2 minutes. Add the shelled shrimp and stir-fry until they become opaque. Add the fish sauce, sugar, and salt, strain in the fish stock and return to a boil.

Divide the scallions and shrimp between 4 deep soup bowls, then ladle in the stock. Add large handfuls of watercress and serve immediately.

*Note: The shrimp shells are included in this recipe because they give terrific flavor. If your shrimp are already shelled, omit this step and stir-fry the ginger, garlic, and lemongrass at the same time as the shrimp, but remove the lemongrass and ginger before serving. You can also use cooked shelled shrimp, adding them at the same time as the stock. For a more substantial soup, add your choice of soaked or fresh noodles with the stock.

2 tablespoons peanut or corn oil

12 uncooked shrimp, peeled but with shells reserved*

1 inch fresh ginger, sliced and crushed

3 garlic cloves, finely sliced

1 stalk lemongrass, halved lengthwise and crushed lightly

1 quart boiling fish stock

8 scallions, white and green, halved crosswise and bruised

2 tablespoons fish sauce, such as Vietnamese *nuóc mam* or Thai *nam pla*

1 tablespoon sugar

1 teaspoon salt

1 large bunch watercress, washed well, dried and trimmed

Serves 4

soups and appetizers

vietnamese
spring rolls

These easy-to-make Vietnamese spring rolls seem fresher and less oily than Chinese. The traditional way of eating them is in a lettuce leaf, topped with grated carrot, bean sprouts, Vietnamese mint, or basil leaves—the package is then rolled up and dipped in *nuóc cham*.

To make *nuóc cham*, work the garlic, chili, and sugar to a purée in a spice grinder. Add the lime flesh and juice and purée again. Transfer to a serving bowl, add about ¼ cup water and the fish sauce, blend well, and set aside.

To make the filling, soak the noodles in hot water for 20 minutes, drain, and snip into short lengths. Soak the mushrooms in boiling water to cover for 30 minutes, then drain and chop. Put the noodles, mushrooms, pork, onion, garlic, scallions, crabmeat, salt, and pepper in a food processor and pulse to mix.

Put 4 rice papers in a bowl of warm water and let soften for 1–2 minutes. Cut each one into 4 wedges. Place 1 wedge on a work surface, put 1 teaspoon of filling next to the curved edge and mold the filling into a small cylinder. Fold that edge over the filling, fold over the two sides like an envelope, then roll up towards the long pointed end. Press to seal. Repeat with all the other wrappers. Fill a wok one-third full of peanut oil and heat to 375°F or until a piece of noodle fluffs up immediately. Put 5–6 spring rolls into the oil and deep-fry until crisp and golden. Remove and drain on paper towels. Repeat until all the spring rolls are cooked. Serve with *nuóc cham* dipping sauce, either plain or with lettuce, bean sprouts, herbs, and grated carrot.

1 oz. cellophane noodles (1 small bundle)

5 Chinese dried cloud ear mushrooms

8 oz. ground pork

½ onion, finely chopped

3 garlic cloves, crushed

3 scallions, finely sliced

5 oz. crabmeat (fresh, frozen, or canned) or chopped shrimp

1 package large Vietnamese rice paper wrappers (50 sheets)*

salt and freshly ground black pepper

peanut or corn oil, for frying

nuóc cham **dipping sauce**

2 garlic cloves, sliced

1 red chili, cored and sliced

1 tablespoon sugar

½ lime, seeded

1½ tablespoons fish sauce, preferably Vietnamese *nuóc mam*

Makes about 40 mini rolls

*The wrappers come in packs of 50 large or 100 small. Wrap leftover wrappers in 2 layers of plastic and seal well. Leftover filling can be made into balls or patties and pan-fried.

indonesian
corn fritters

A great vegetarian treat for adults or children (use peppers instead of chilies if serving to children). Their Indonesian name is *frikadel*, similar to the German, Scandinavian, and Dutch words for "rissole"—a legacy of the colonial Dutch rule in the former Spice Islands.

Mix the corn in a bowl with the fish sauce, Szechuan pepper, chilies, and scallions. Stir in the beaten eggs and cornstarch.

Heat 2 tablespoons oil in a wok or skillet and swirl to coat the surface. Drop in a large spoonful of the corn mixture and let cook for 2 minutes until it begins to bubble around the edges. Check that the underside is golden, then turn it over and lightly brown the other side.

Remove to a plate covered with crumpled paper towels and put in a warm oven while you make the remaining fritters.

Transfer the fritters to a platter and serve with a dip such as peanut sauce, chili dipping sauce, or Vietnamese *nuóc cham*.

*Note: If using fresh corn, hold the cobs, blunt side down, on a board and run a knife downward, shaving off the kernels. About 4 medium cobs should produce 1 lb. of kernels. You can also include chopped, shelled shrimp in this mixture and reduce the quantity of corn by half.

1 lb. fresh, canned, or frozen
   corn kernels*
2 tablespoons fish sauce, such as
   Vietnamese *nuóc mam* or Thai *nam pla*
1 tablespoon Szechuan peppercorns (or
   black peppercorns), crushed
2 medium red chilies, cored and diced
8 scallions, thickly sliced crosswise into
   pea-sized chunks
2 eggs, beaten
4 tablespoons cornstarch
corn or peanut oil, for frying

to serve (optional)
peanut sauce (page 62), chili dipping
   sauce (page 28), or *nuóc cham* (page 11)
Serves 4

chinese dim sum
steamed dumplings

Fellow food writer Clare Ferguson serves great party food—this is a pork variation on her traditional chicken version of these *dim sum* dumplings.

Put the pork, shrimp, and bacon into a food processor and blend to a purée. With the motor running, add the Szechuan pepper, egg white, sesame oil, ginger, salt, garlic, and cornstarch.

Finely chop the white and green parts of the scallions crosswise, transfer to a mixing bowl, add the pork mixture, water chestnuts, and sliced beans. Mix well. Cut the square wonton wrappers into rounds with a knife or cookie cutter, then put 1 tablespoon filling in the center of each. Use a small spatula to smooth the mixture almost to the edges.

Cup the wonton in the palm of your hand. Gather up your hand, pushing down with the spatula—you will achieve an open-topped, pleated, purse-shaped container filled with mixture. Drop it gently onto a floured surface to flatten the bottom and settle the filling. Repeat until all the dumplings are made.

Set on several racks of a steamer, lined with banana leaves or parchment paper. Put the steamer in a wok with simmering water at least 1 inch below the base of the steamer. Cover and steam for about 7–10 minutes, refilling the base with boiling water as necessary. Serve hot with a simple dip of soy sauce.

Note: This is great party food—you can steam the dumplings in layers and serve them straight from the pretty bamboo steamers. Cook 3 tiers at a time, and have the next 3 tiers cooking while you serve the first.

1 lb. ground pork

4 oz. shelled shrimp

3 slices smoked bacon, chopped

1 teaspoon crushed Szechuan pepper

1 egg white

2 teaspoons sesame oil

1 inch fresh ginger, grated

2 teaspoons sea salt flakes

2 fat garlic cloves, crushed

2 teaspoons cornstarch

4 scallions

4 canned water chestnuts, finely diced

4 Chinese long beans, finely sliced

1–2 packages wonton wrappers*

soy sauce, to serve

Serves 10

*Packages vary, but most contain about 40 large (4-inch) or 70 small (3–inch) wrappers. Leftover wrappers can be frozen.

vietnamese pâté
with pork and noodles

3–4 large pieces dried black fungus

1 oz. bean thread vermicelli noodles
   (1 small bundle)

4 slices bacon (optional)

1 lb. ground pork

1 onion, finely chopped

3–6 fat garlic cloves, crushed with salt

1 tablespoon sugar

3 tablespoons fish sauce (*nuóc mam*)

1 tablespoon Szechuan peppercorns or
   black peppercorns, coarsely crushed

3 large eggs, beaten

2–4 red chilies, finely sliced (optional)

2 egg yolks, beaten with 1 tablespoon
   sunflower oil (optional—see note)*

Serves 4

The French colonial period made the Vietnamese masterly bakers (some of the best bread in Australia and America is produced by Vietnamese émigrés). Pâtés, too, show French influence, albeit with a decidedly local emphasis.

Put the fungus in a heatproof bowl and cover with boiling water. Let stand for about 10 minutes, drain, squeeze dry in a cloth, and chop coarsely. (Remove the hard center stem first.) Put the noodles in a heatproof bowl and cover with hot water. Let stand for about 5 minutes, drain, and chop into 3-inch lengths. Stir-fry the bacon, if using, until crisp. Put the pork, onion, garlic, sugar, fish sauce, pepper, bacon, and beaten eggs in a food processor and blend until smooth. Transfer to a bowl and mix in the noodles, fungus, and chilies, if using. Brush a container such as a loaf pan, terrine, or 8–9 inch soufflé dish with oil. Spoon in the mixture and cover with banana leaf or foil. Tie string around the top and steam over a wok of simmering water for 25–50 minutes (depending on the size of the dish). Top up with extra boiling water as required. Test by putting a chopstick into the center of the pâté. If liquid shows in the hole, cook it longer. Serve with other Asian dishes, or in baguettes with lettuce and mint as shown. Like most pâtés, this one is very good chilled and served the next day.

*Note: The pâté is also very easy to make when cooked in a microwave at 30–35% power for about 15–20 minutes. Test as above.
For a golden topping for the cooked pâté, beat 2 egg yolks with 1 tablespoon oil and brush evenly over the surface. Steam for a few minutes until the egg sets.

chinese crispy
deep-fried wontons

I love wontons—they're easy to make and you can vary the fillings, using shrimp, crabmeat, or chicken. They make spectacular party food—serve them with a simple soy sauce dip or a chili dip for your hothead friends!

4 oz. ground pork

4 garlic cloves, crushed

salt and pepper

4 water chestnuts, chopped

1–2 packages wonton wrappers*

1 egg, beaten

1 bunch Chinese chives (optional)

soy sauce, to serve (optional)

peanut or corn oil, for frying

dipping sauce (optional)

¼ cup soy sauce

1 red chili, sliced

1 scallion, finely sliced

1 tablespoon rice vinegar

Serves 4

*Packages vary, but most contain about 40 large (4-inch) or 70 small (3-inch) wrappers. Leftover wrappers can be frozen.

Put the ground pork into a food processor with the garlic, salt, and pepper and blend until smooth. Transfer to a bowl and mix in the chopped water chestnuts or bamboo shoots.

Mix the dipping sauce ingredients in a bowl and put on a serving platter.

Take the wonton wrappers out of the plastic bag, but keep them covered with plastic as you work, because they dry out quickly.

Place 1 wonton wrapper on the work surface and put 1 tablespoon of filling in the middle. Brush a circle of beaten egg around the filling, pull up the sides of the wrapper and twirl the free part of the pastry close up against the ball of filling, so you have a frilly top. Open out the frill. You can tie a blanched chive around the seam if you like, but the egg acts as glue.

When all the wontons are assembled, fill the wok one-third full of oil and heat to about 375°F or until a piece of noodle fluffs up immediately.

Add the wontons, 3–4 at a time, and deep-fry for a few minutes on each side until brown and crisp. Do not let the oil get too hot, or the wonton pastry will cook before the filling.

Transfer to a plate covered with crumpled paper towels to drain while you cook the remaining wontons (skim any debris from the oil between batches).

Serve hot, with the dipping sauce and a small dish of plain soy sauce for the less fiery personalities among your guests!

fish and seafood

japanese steamed fish
on buckwheat noodles with seaweed

This is a very elegant and stylish dish, and easy to make —the bowls can be assembled beforehand, then cooked at the very last minute. The traditional Japanese practice of salting the fish increases the succulence of its flesh when cooked—a great secret for all fish cooks!

1 salmon fillet, about 1–1½ lb.

1 bundle (4 oz.) soba buckwheat noodles, or green tea noodles

1 sheet kombu seaweed, cut into 4 pieces (optional)*

4 tablespoons sake or Chinese rice wine

dashi sauce

1 cup dashi stock

¾ cup mirin or ginger wine

¾ cup Japanese soy sauce

1 handful dried bonito flakes (optional)

Serves 4

Cut the salmon crosswise into 4 strips and put the pieces, skin side down, on a plate sprinkled with a layer of salt. Set aside for 20 minutes, then quickly rinse off the salt and pat dry with paper towels.

Bring a large saucepan of water to a boil, add the noodles, and cook, stirring a little with chopsticks, until the water returns to a boil. Add a splash of cold water and return to a boil. Repeat this 2 more times, until the noodles are *al dente*—a total of 3–4 minutes. Drain, rinse in cold water, and set aside.

When ready to assemble, dip the noodles into boiling water and drain. Put pieces of seaweed, if using, into 4 lidded china bowls (to fit into 1 or more tiers of a bamboo steamer). Add a pile of noodles and top with a fish fillet, skin side up. Sprinkle 1 tablespoon sake or rice wine over each one, put a circle of foil on top and the lid on top of that. Put the steamer into the wok, pour in boiling water to about 1 inch below the base, cover, and steam for 10 minutes or until done. Put the dashi sauce ingredients into a saucepan, bring to a boil and, when ready to serve, strain over the fish. Serve with chopsticks. Heavenly!

Note: The kombu seaweed is there for flavor—discard before eating.

chinese steamed fish
with southeast asian variations

Chinese cooks are very discerning in choosing their fish—they like a fine-textured fish with good flavor for this dish. I use grouper, but moonfish, butterfish, coral cod, parrot fish, red snapper, or sea bass are also good.

1 large whole fish, such as grouper, sea
    bass, or snapper, about 2 lb., cleaned
    and scaled*

2 inches fresh ginger, very finely sliced

3 garlic cloves, crushed

6 scallions, finely sliced lengthwise

1 tablespoon corn or peanut oil,
    for brushing

2 tablespoons soy sauce

2 tablespoons rice wine, dry sherry,
    or ginger wine

Serves 4

*Take the lid of the steamer with you when
you buy the fish, to make sure it will fit.

Rinse the fish in salted water, then pat dry with paper towels. Stuff the cavity with ginger, garlic, and half the scallions, and brush the skin with oil.

Put the fish on a plate and put the plate into a steamer. Sprinkle with the soy sauce and rice wine. Put the steamer into a wok one-third full of boiling water. Simmer, steaming, until the fish is opaque (the time will depend on the thickness of the fish, but about 20–30 minutes is usual).

Blanch the remaining scallions in boiling water for 10 seconds, then drain. Remove the steamer from the wok, then remove the plate from the steamer. Scatter the blanched scallions over the fish and serve with other Chinese dishes. (I always discard the flavorings from the cavity before serving.)

Note: It is regarded as bad luck to turn the fish over. Serve it from one side of the bone, then remove and discard the bone and serve the remaining fish. You can also bone the fish before serving, reassembling it carefully on the plate.

To add a Thai flavor, add 1 stalk finely chopped lemongrass and 1 teaspoon tamarind paste thinned with 1 tablespoon boiling water before steaming.

For a Vietnamese accent, add 1 tablespoon fish sauce and 1 teaspoon brown sugar to the sauce before steaming.

For Lao steamed fish, heat 1 teaspoon shrimp paste (or 1 anchovy fillet mashed with 1 teaspoon water) for 1 minute. Stir into the soy sauce before steaming.

japanese tempura

2 onions, halved through the root

1 lb. white fish, cut into bite-sized strips

8 shrimp, shelled, with tail fins intact

8 baby squid, cleaned (optional)

2 orange sweet potatoes, finely sliced

4 sheets nori seaweed (optional)

10 shiso leaves (optional)

1 cup all-purpose flour, for dredging

corn or peanut oil, for frying

tempura batter

¼ cup cornstarch

¾ cup all-purpose flour

1 teaspoon baking powder

5 teaspoons corn or peanut oil

¾ cup club soda water

dashi dip

¾ cup dashi stock*

⅛ cup mirin (Chinese rice wine)

⅛ cup light Japanese soy sauce

1 inch Japanese white daikon (mooli),
   coarsely grated

1 inch fresh ginger, grated

Serves 4

Tempura batter provides a light and lacy coating. The mixture must be lumpy and mixed with chopsticks just before cooking—do not let it rest. The cooking-and-serving process must be quick and efficient.

Cut the onion halves crosswise into thick half-rings, keeping the segments together with toothpicks. Pat all the seafood, vegetables, seaweed, and leaves dry, pressing out any liquid from the shrimp (I prefer them halved lengthwise, but please yourself). Mix the dashi dip ingredients together and set aside.

Put a shallow dish of flour to your left and a bowl for the batter to the right of that. Fill the wok one-third full of oil, and heat to 375°F, or until a piece of noodle fluffs up immediately. Put tongs or chopsticks to your right, and a serving platter lined with crumpled paper towels to the right of that.

Put the batter ingredients into the bowl and mix quickly with chopsticks, leaving as lumpy as possible. Working first with the onion half-rings and sweet potato, dip each piece in the batter, then slide it into the hot oil and fry until the batter is golden. Remove with tongs or chopsticks to the plate of paper towels. Each piece is cooked only until the batter is golden.

Increase the heat and cook the fish first, then the squid and shrimp. If using the seaweed and shiso leaves, dip one side only in the batter before frying. Remove, drain, and serve immediately with the dipping sauce.

*****Note:** Dashi is sold in powder or concentrate form, or you can make your own by simmering kombu seaweed, grated dried bonito, and water, then straining.

japanese sea bream
sautéed with sake-butter sauce

This is a quick and simple dish—and you don't even need the traditional first step, although the fish will have better texture if you do. The result is very elegant and the taste absolutely mind-blowing. Using butter in an Asian dish is unusual, and shows how many cuisines are constantly influenced by the foods of other countries.

Pat the fish dry on paper towels. Sprinkle a layer of salt on a plate, put the fish on top, skin side down, and set aside for 20 minutes while you prepare the other ingredients. When ready to cook, rinse the salt off the fish and pat dry.
Heat a wok until very hot, then brush with a little oil and heat until smoking. Add the fish, skin side down, and press it down with a spatula. Cook about 1 minute on high heat, then turn over the fish and cook it for about 2 minutes on the other side.
Remove the fish from the wok to a heated dish and rinse out the wok. Return it to the heat, add the butter, return the fish to the wok, and turn it to coat in the butter. Transfer the fish to serving plates, add the remaining ingredients to the wok, and boil fiercely for 1 minute. Pour over the fish and serve immediately.

Note: This recipe is endlessly adaptable. It can be served with other Japanese dishes, or served in the Western way with vegetables of your choice.
Japanese 7-spice (*shichimi togarishi*) may be difficult to find—Szechuan pepper or ordinary freshly ground black pepper may be used instead.

4–8 fish fillets (not cutlets), such as red sea bream, red snapper, salmon, or sea bass, well scaled (6 oz. per serving)
sea salt (see method)
2 tablespoons peanut oil
4 tablespoons (½ stick) unsalted butter
6 scallions, finely sliced crosswise
1 inch fresh ginger, sliced lengthwise
1 teaspoon Japanese 7-spice, ground Szechuan peppercorns, or freshly ground black pepper
½ cup rice vinegar
½ cup sake, Chinese rice wine, or ginger wine
2 tablespoons Japanese soy sauce
Serves 4

thai crabcakes
with chili dipping sauce

There are a million recipes for Thai crab or fishcakes. Chopped green beans are popular with Western chefs, but I prefer Chinese long beans—they have better texture, more interesting taste, and keep their form through thick and thin.

3 red chilies, cored

3 scallions, finely sliced

2 garlic cloves, crushed

4 cilantro stalks, finely chopped

1 inch fresh galangal or ginger, chopped

6 kaffir lime leaves, finely sliced

1 tablespoon fish sauce

8 oz. boneless fish fillets, such as cod

8 oz. crabmeat (fresh, frozen, or canned)

2 Chinese long beans, finely sliced

1 oz. beanthread (cellophane) noodles

1 egg, beaten

2 tablespoons peanut oil, for frying

chili dipping sauce

½ cup white rice vinegar

1 red chili, finely sliced

1 tablespoon fish sauce, such as *nam pla*

1 scallion, finely sliced

1 teaspoon brown sugar

Serves 4

Put the chilies, scallions, garlic, cilantro stalks, galangal or ginger, fish sauce, and kaffir lime leaves in a food processor and work to a paste. Add the fish and work to a paste. Transfer to a bowl and mix in the crab and beans.

Soak the beanthread noodles in a bowl of hot water for 5 minutes, then drain and scissor-snip into short (about 1 inch) pieces. Mix into the fish and stir in the beaten egg. Wet your hands with water and shape the mixture into flat hamburger-shaped patties of about 3 tablespoons each.

Heat the oil in a wok and swirl to coat the sides. Add the crabcakes, 3 at a time, and sauté until golden. Transfer to a plate lined with crumpled paper towels and keep them hot in the oven while you cook the remaining crabcakes.

Mix the dipping sauce ingredients together and serve 3 crabcakes per person with a small bowl of the sauce and a tangle of fresh salad leaves.

Note: The crabcakes can also be deep-fried in a wok about one-third full of oil. If you can find it, use pretty, pink-tipped galangal root with its spicy soda-pop flavor. It is a cousin of ginger, which can be used instead. The patties can also be sprinkled with rice flour before cooking.

thai baby squid

with green curry paste

Buy red or green Thai curry paste in larger supermarkets or Asian stores.
I freeze it in ice cube trays, then keep the cubes in labeled plastic bags in the
freezer—then the perfect amount is always on hand, ready for each dish.

2 lb. whole baby squid, or 1½ lb. cleaned*

2 tablespoons corn or peanut oil

1 tablespoon green curry paste

1 tablespoon freshly squeezed lime juice

grated zest of 1 lime, preferably kaffir lime

1 tablespoon fish sauce, such as *nam pla*

a pinch of sugar

sprigs of cilantro, to serve

Serves 4

***Note: If you're squeamish about cleaning
squid (really very easy), you can buy it ready-
cleaned. You will miss out on the pretty
tentacles, but it will still taste great.**

If using whole squid, pull the tentacles away from the hood—the head and
insides will come away with them. Cut the tentacles away from the head and
discard it. Rinse the inside of the squid, and remove the transparent quill. (Leave
on the purple skin—it tastes great and looks pretty.) Cut the hood down one side
and open it out, skin side down. Using a Chinese cleaver or sharp knife, make
lines diagonally across the hood, without cutting right through. Turn the hood
90 degrees and repeat, making a diamond pattern. Set aside.

Heat the oil in a wok, add the green curry paste, and stir-fry for 1 minute. Add
the diamond cut hoods and tentacles and stir-fry for 1 minute. Add the lime
juice, lime zest, fish sauce, and sugar and stir-fry for a few seconds. Serve with
sprigs of cilantro. Boiled fragrant Thai rice is a suitable accompaniment.

vietnamese
shaking beef

This quivering recipe gets its name from the spectacular pan-tossing technique experienced chefs use when stir-frying.

Mix 4 of the garlic cloves, the fish sauce, sugar, a pinch of salt, and half the oil in a bowl, add the beef, and toss until well coated. Cover and set aside to marinate in the refrigerator for at least 30 minutes.

Put the onion in a bowl, cover with vinegar, and let stand for 10 minutes. Add the sesame oil, salt, and pepper and set aside.

Heat the remaining oil in a wok, add the remaining garlic, stir-fry for 1 minute, then add the beef and chilies, if using. Stir-fry or toss quickly over a high heat until the meat is brown and crisp on the outside and rare in the middle.

Transfer the onion to a serving plate and drizzle the dressing over the top. Serve the beef on top or beside. Crisp salad leaves are a suitable accompaniment, as with many Vietnamese recipes.

This dish should accompany other dishes, including rice, vegetables, and perhaps a seafood dish.

5 garlic cloves, chopped

1 tablespoon fish sauce, such as Thai *nam pla* or Vietnamese *nuóc mam*

1 teaspoon brown sugar or palm sugar

2 tablespoons peanut oil

1 lb. boneless sirloin cut into 1-inch cubes

1 onion, halved and finely sliced

1 tablespoon rice vinegar

1 teaspoon sesame oil

2–6 green chilies, sliced crosswise (optional)

salt and freshly ground black pepper

Serves 4

meat and poultry

thai marinated chicken
stir-fried in chili oil

I prefer the meat from the thigh of the chicken, because I think it has more flavor, and if you cook it on the bone, that too seems to give it more flavor. However, I must admit that stir-fries are infinitely easier with boneless pieces of meat, so use boneless breasts or thighs, cut into 1-inch thick slices.

8 boneless chicken thighs or 4 breasts

3 teaspoons turmeric

3 whole star anise, crushed

3 garlic cloves, crushed

2 inches fresh ginger, finely sliced

grated zest of 1 lime or 2 kaffir limes
    and 1 tablespoon lime juice

2 tablespoons fish sauce

1 tablespoon dark soy sauce

2 tablespoons chili oil

1 tablespoon peanut oil

5 Chinese long beans, cut into 2-inch
    lengths (optional)

2 cups coconut milk

sliced red chilies, to serve

Serves 4

Place the chicken, skin side down, in a shallow non-reactive container. To marinate, rub in the turmeric, star anise, garlic, ginger, and lime zest, then sprinkle with the fish sauce, soy sauce, half the chili oil, and lime juice. Turn the chicken pieces in the mixture to coat well, cover, and leave in the refrigerator to marinate for 1 hour or overnight, turning at least once.

When ready to cook, drain, slice into ½-inch strips and reserve the marinade. Heat the wok, add the peanut oil and remaining chili oil, and heat until hot, then add the chicken pieces, skin side down. Cook at a high heat for 1–2 minutes until the skin is crispy, then turn down the heat and continue cooking until browned. Turn the pieces over and brown the other side.

Add the beans, reserved marinade, and the coconut milk. Stir well. Bring to a boil, stirring slowly; lower the heat and simmer for 10–15 minutes until the chicken is tender. Sprinkle with sliced red chili and serve.

Fragrant Thai rice and a vegetable dish would be suitable accompaniments.

lao chicken and ginger
in coconut milk or coconut water

The cooking of Laos is only just becoming known in the US, though in my native Australia, Lao immigrants have already introduced their recipes to an avid local audience. In the original dish, a whole chicken is stuffed with peanuts, then stewed in coconut milk or water—but I like it without the nuts!

2–4 tablespoons corn or peanut oil

6 shallots or 4 onions, sliced

2 inches fresh ginger, sliced and diced

3–6 garlic cloves, crushed

8–12 chicken thighs, with skin

2 medium-hot chilies, red or green, cored
and sliced, plus extra to serve

1 teaspoon brown sugar

1 tablespoon fish sauce such as *nam pla*,
or 1 teaspoon *blachan* (shrimp paste)

2 cups coconut water or coconut milk*

8 oz. pea eggplants (optional) or cooked
green peas

6 scallions, halved then finely
sliced lengthwise

10 large cilantro sprigs

Serves 4

Heat the oil in a wok, add the shallots or onions, and stir-fry until golden. Add the ginger and garlic and stir-fry for 1–2 minutes. Remove to a plate, then add the chicken to the wok, and sauté on all sides until golden. Stir in the onion mixture, chilies, sugar, and fish sauce or shrimp paste (wrap paste in foil and broil for 1 minute first, or put in a covered bowl and cook for 1 minute in a microwave). Add the coconut water, bring to a boil, reduce the heat, and cover with a lid—if using coconut milk, don't put on a lid or the milk will curdle. Simmer gently for about 20 minutes, or until the chicken is tender.

If using coconut milk, bring it gently to a boil (stirring, or it will curdle), then reduce the heat and simmer until the chicken is done.

Add the pea eggplants or peas, simmer for 2 minutes, then serve topped with scallions, cilantro, and chilies, plus fragrant Thai rice—in Laos, it would be glutinous rice, rolled up with the chicken, dipped in sauce, then eaten with the fingers.

*Note: Coconut water (not milk) is the almost-clear liquid inside the nut and gives a sweet scent to this dish. It may be hard to find outside coconut-growing areas, but you can buy it in cartons or cans in the fruit drinks section of Asian or Caribbean stores (omit the sugar, because the drink will have been sweetened). Pea eggplants, like bunches of mini-grapes, are sold in Thai and Asian stores.

thai pork balls
with chili dipping sauce

A delicious entrée served with other Asian dishes, and also great at cocktail parties. Use fat Fresno chilies for a mild flavor, or bird's eye chilies for blinding heat.

1 lb. ground pork

6 garlic cloves, crushed

2 stalks lemongrass, finely sliced

1 bunch cilantro, finely chopped

2 fresh red chilies, cored and diced

1 tablespoon brown sugar

1 tablespoon fish sauce, such as *nam pla*

1 egg, beaten

salt and freshly ground black pepper

peanut oil, for frying

chili dipping sauce

½ cup white rice vinegar

2–6 small or 1 large red chili, finely sliced

1 tablespoon fish sauce

1 scallion, finely sliced (optional)

½–1 tablespoon brown sugar

Serves 4

Mix all the ingredients for the chili dipping sauce in a small bowl, stir to dissolve the sugar, then set aside to develop the flavors.

To make the pork balls, place all the remaining ingredients, except the peanut oil, in a bowl and mix well. Dip your hands in water, take about 1–2 tablespoons of the mixture, and roll it into a ball. Repeat with the remaining mixture.

Fill a wok one-third full of peanut oil and heat until a cube of bread browns in 30 seconds. Add the pork balls, 6 at a time, and deep-fry in batches until golden brown. Remove and drain on crumpled paper towels, keeping them warm in the oven until all the balls are done. Serve with the chili dipping sauce.

cambodian spareribs
with sugar-lime sauce

Ask the butcher to chop the spareribs into short sections for you. It's possible to do this yourself, using a Chinese cleaver, but infinitely safer to ask an expert to do it instead. A friend of mine found this recipe in Cambodia, but I have hybridized it by adding a Vietnamese sweet-and-sour dipping sauce and the light, crisp, Japanese tempura batter on page 24. This is a hands-on dish, so provide lots of steaming hot towels for mopping up!

1 tablespoon soy sauce

juice of 1 lime

1 tablespoon sugar

2 lb. pork spareribs, cut in 2-inch lengths

1 quantity tempura batter (page 24)

1 cup all-purpose flour, for dredging

sea salt flakes, to serve

corn or peanut oil, for frying

sugar-lime sauce

2 tablespoons lime juice
   or white rice vinegar

½ cup brown sugar

Serves 4

Put the soy sauce, lime juice, and sugar in a shallow dish, add the ribs and turn to coat. Cover and chill for about 30 minutes to marinate.

Heat the sauce ingredients in a saucepan or wok until the sugar dissolves, and keep the mixture warm until ready to serve.

Put the dry tempura batter ingredients into a bowl, but do not add the liquids until just before cooking the ribs. Put the flour on a flat plate.

Fill a wok one-third full of oil and heat until a cube of bread browns in 30 seconds. Quickly mix the batter with chopsticks (don't mix too well—there should be a rim of flour around the bowl).

In batches of 5–6, dip the ribs into the flour to coat, shake off the excess, then dip them in the batter. Put into the hot oil and cook until golden brown.

Remove the ribs as they are ready, drain on crumpled paper towels, and keep them warm in the oven while you cook the remainder.

Serve sprinkled with sea salt and drizzled with sugar-lime sauce.

tea-smoked
chinese duck

Tea-smoking is great for fish and poultry. Smoking over tea leaves and sugar gives a wonderful taste, and the food need not be cooked after smoking, though I do like to char-grill the duck for extra flavor.

Rub the duck breasts with chili oil and 5-spice powder and use immediately, or put in a bowl, cover, and chill for up to 24 hours to develop the flavors.

When ready to cook, put a double layer of foil in the wok, overlapping the edges. Put the tea leaves, flour, sugar, orange or tangerine peel, and star anise in the bottom. Put a round smoking rack or cake rack on top, and the duck, skin-side up, on top of that. Cover with more foil, then cover tightly with a lid.

Heat the wok until the smoke rises. Keep smoking for about 15 minutes, then turn the duck over and continue smoking for a further 15 minutes or until done. Remove the duck and serve immediately, or char-grill, skin-side down, on a stove-top grill pan for a few minutes for extra flavor.

The duck may be sliced and served with rice and vegetables, or as part of a combination noodle dish. It is also delicious served in the Western manner with sautéed or steamed vegetables.

Note: This is an opportunity to use one of the wonderful Chinese or Japanese teas, including jasmine tea, gunpowder green tea, orange pekoe, Japanese green tea, or even Earl Grey. The difference in flavor is probably minimal, but I must admit it adds to the fun!

4 small duck breasts

2 tablespoons chili oil

4 teaspoons Chinese 5-spice powder

8 tablespoons Chinese tea leaves

2 tablespoons all-purpose flour

1 tablespoon brown sugar

1 strip fresh orange peel or 6 pieces dried tangerine peel

4–6 whole star anise

Serves 4

vietnamese pho ca
chicken noodle soup

Pho (pronounced "far") is the comfort food of Vietnam, eaten at any time of day. The first requirement is good stock, simmered for hours. Being lazy, I buy my stock and simmer it for a few minutes with Vietnamese aromatics.

1 packet fresh **banh pho** or **ho fun** noodles
  or dried rice sticks

1 tablespoon peanut oil

2 boneless chicken breasts, finely sliced

1 tablespoon brown sugar

2 tablespoons fish sauce (**nuóc mam**)

chicken stock

2 quarts chicken stock

4 whole star anise

2 inches fresh ginger, sliced or chopped

2 onions, cut into wedges

1 cinnamon stick

to serve

your choice of scallions, bean sprouts,
  sprigs of cilantro and Asian basil, sliced
  red chilies, lime wedges, and sliced
  romaine lettuce (not traditional)

Serves 4

Put the stock ingredients into a saucepan, bring to a boil, and simmer gently for about 30 minutes to extract the flavors (or boil hard for 10 minutes, but don't allow it to evaporate).

If using dried rice sticks, soak in hot water for 15 minutes, then drain.

Heat the oil in a wok, add the chicken, sugar, and fish sauce and stir-fry for 1–2 minutes until done.

Dip the noodles, whether fresh or dried and soaked, in boiling water for about 1 minute to heat through, then drain and divide between 4 large bowls. Put the chicken on top and strain over the stock. Serve with your choice of serving ingredients on a separate serving plate (to be added to taste).

rice and
noodles

singapore
coconut laksa

Laksas are one-bowl meals from Malaysia and Singapore. The spice paste usually contains candlenuts (we had a huge tree outside the house where I grew up), but if you can't find any, use almonds or macadamias instead.

1 quart coconut milk (about 4 cans)

8 oz. somen or cellophane noodles

4 tablespoons peanut oil

1 lb. boneless chicken, cut in ½-inch strips

1 small package bean sprouts, trimmed

4 scallions, sliced diagonally

1 red chili, cored and finely sliced

sprigs of mint and cilantro

sea salt, to taste

spice paste

4 red or orange chilies (not habaneros)

3 stalks lemongrass, finely sliced

1 inch fresh galangal or ginger, sliced

1 teaspoon ground turmeric*

4 candlenuts or 8 almonds, crushed

1 teaspoon *blachan* (shrimp paste)*

1 garlic clove, chopped

4 shallots or 2 mild onions, sliced

1 tablespoon coriander seeds

Serves 4

Open the cans of coconut milk and pour the thick and thin bits into separate bowls. Put all the spice paste ingredients into a spice grinder (I use a coffee grinder) and work to a mush, in batches if necessary.

If using somen noodles, cook in boiling salted water for 2½–3 minutes. Add a splash of cold water from time to time, then return to a boil. If using cellophane noodles, soak in hot water for 15 minutes, then boil for 1 minute before serving. Heat the oil in a wok, add the chicken, and stir-fry until lightly golden and cooked through. Remove from the wok and set aside. Add the spice paste and cook, stirring until aromatic—about 6–8 minutes.

Add the thin coconut milk, bring to a boil, stirring, add the cooked chicken, and return to a boil, still stirring. Add the thick part of the coconut milk and cook gently, stirring, until well heated (keep stirring or the coconut milk will curdle). Serve in large soup bowls with sprigs of mint and cilantro.

*Note: Beautiful fresh turmeric roots are sold in Thai shops and give wonderful color and flavor. Peel and slice before using instead of ground turmeric.
Shrimp paste is sold in Asian stores, and must be either covered and heated in a microwave first, or wrapped in foil and broiled for a few minutes. If unavailable, use a similar quantity of Thai or Vietnamese fish sauce, or anchovy essence.

malaysian penang
tamarind fish laksa

Make spice pastes in quantity and freeze them—this one, the previous one, or a ready-made Thai curry paste are all good. Tamarind gives this laksa a lemony taste.

If using dried noodles, cook in boiling salted water for 10–12 minutes; if fresh, boil for 2–2½ minutes. During boiling, add a splash of cold water once or twice during the cooking time, then return to a boil. Drain and cover with cold water until ready to assemble the dish.

Put all the spice paste ingredients, except the peanut oil, in a blender, spice grinder, or small food processor and work to a purée, adding a few tablespoons of water as necessary to make a paste. Heat the oil in a wok, add the paste, and stir-fry for about 6 minutes—the rawness should be cooked out of the spices. Add the stock and ginger and heat until boiling, add the fish, turn off the heat, and put on the lid. Leave for about 5 minutes until the fish is cooked, then break the fish into large pieces in the stock. Reheat to boiling point, then stir in the tamarind paste, sugar, salt, and pepper.

Drain the noodles, then dunk them and the shrimp, if using, into boiling water until heated through. Drain, then put a pile of the hot noodles in 4 large Chinese soup bowls, ladle the fish and stock over the top, and sprinkle with mint, bean sprouts, shrimp, cilantro, and chilies.

*Note: Tamarind paste is sold in bottles in Asian shops, and I think this is the most convenient form. Substitute the juice of 1 lime if you can't find it.

1 lb. fresh udon noodles, or 8 oz. dried

1 quart fish stock or water

1 inch fresh ginger or galangal, grated

1 lb. skinless, boneless fish fillets

1 tablespoon tamarind paste*

1 teaspoon brown sugar or palm sugar

sea salt and freshly ground black pepper

spice paste

3 dried chilies, cored and soaked

2 stalks lemongrass, chopped

1 inch fresh ginger or galangal, grated

1 teaspoon turmeric (see note page 47)

1 tablespoon *blachan* (shrimp paste)

12 scallions, finely sliced

1 tablespoon peanut oil

to serve

8–12 cooked, peeled shrimp (optional)

1 bunch Vietnamese mint or mint

1 small package bean sprouts, trimmed

1 bunch cilantro leaves, torn

2 red chilies, cored and finely sliced

Serves 4

thai mee krob

This is the easiest and most delicious noodle dish in the world! Don't worry about deep-frying the noodles—they quickly puff up in a most satisfying fashion.

4 bundles dried wide ricestick noodles or
    fine rice vermicelli noodles*
peanut oil, for frying

dressing
½ cup white rice vinegar
⅔ cup palm sugar or brown sugar
¼ cup soy sauce
¼ cup fish sauce, such as *nam pla*

toppings
1 tablespoon vegetable oil
1 tablespoon mussaman curry paste*
4 pork chops, boned and sliced
4–8 uncooked shrimp, peeled, tail fins
    intact, halved lengthwise
8 scallions, sliced diagonally
6 baby Thai shallots, sliced (optional)
1 small package bean sprouts, trimmed
2 red chilies, cored and sliced crosswise
sprigs of cilantro
Serves 4

Mix the dressing ingredients together in a small saucepan and cook, stirring, just until dissolved. Keep hot. Line 4 serving bowls with crumpled paper towels. To make the toppings, heat the oil in a wok, add the curry paste, and cook for 1–2 minutes until you cough (that means the aromatics have been released). Add the pork strips and stir-fry until crisp, add the shrimp, and stir-fry for about 1 minute until they turn opaque. Transfer to a dish and keep them warm.

Wipe out the wok, fill one-third full of oil, and heat to 375°F or until a small piece of noodle fluffs up immediately.

Add a handful of noodles—let puff and cook for 1 minute, then carefully turn over with tongs and cook the other side for 1 minute. Remove to one of the paper-lined bowls. Reheat the oil and repeat with the remaining noodles, reheating and skimming the oil as necessary. When all are ready, turn the noodles over in the bowls and discard the paper. Divide the toppings between each bowl, drizzle over the dressing, and serve with chopsticks.

*Note: Fine noodles are traditional for this recipe, but the wide ones are fun, and are great party nibbles when deep-fried and sprinkled with salt and chili powder. Mild orange mussaman curry paste is sold in larger supermarkets and Thai shops. If unavailable, use another Thai curry paste, such as red or green.

banana leaf packages
with rice, bacon, and egg

This is an easy version of a more complicated traditional recipe. Other leaves, such as lotus or pandan, may be used instead, as can a simple foil package, perhaps with pieces of banana, lotus, pandan, or bay leaves added for flavor.

4 dried shiitake mushrooms

10 oz. jasmine rice

1 inch fresh ginger, sliced

a pinch of salt

2 tablespoons peanut oil

8 slices smoked bacon, sliced crosswise

2 eggs

4 fresh banana leaves, or dried lotus
   leaves, soaked in boiling water
   until supple

flavor mixture

1 tablespoon rice wine or ginger wine

1 tablespoon dark soy sauce

1 tablespoon oyster sauce

a pinch of sugar

1 teaspoon sesame oil

Serves 4

Put the mushrooms in a bowl, cover with boiling water, and soak for 30 minutes. Drain, discard the stems, and finely slice the caps.

Mix the ingredients for the flavor mixture in a small bowl and set aside.

Put the rice and ginger in a saucepan, add enough water to come 1 inch above the top of the rice. Add a pinch of salt, bring to a boil, cover, and cook for 8 minutes until the rice is part-cooked. Drain and discard the ginger.

Heat the oil in a wok, add the bacon, and stir-fry until crisp. Remove and set aside. Beat the eggs in a bowl with 1 tablespoon water. Reheat the bacon fat in the wok and swirl it so the sides are well coated (add a little oil if necessary). Add the beaten eggs and swirl around the wok so the eggs form a thin omelet. Cook until just set, shake the wok so the omelet turns over on itself, then turn out onto a plate and slice it finely.

Open out the banana or lotus leaves, put a pile of rice in the middle and a share of all the other ingredients, including the flavor mixture. Fold up into square packages, tie with string or thread, and place in a bamboo steamer set over a wok of boiling water. Steam for 20 minutes, then serve, cutting a cross in the top of each package just before serving so the aromas escape across the table.

Note: Other ingredients may also be added to the rice, such as cooked shredded duck, chicken, or stir-fried pork strips.

chinese mushrooms
with cilantro, mint, or basil

There are so many cultivated mushrooms available now that it seems a pity not to take advantage of them in stir-fries, where their form, color, and flavor is shown off to best advantage. A wonderful mixture is cooked here with the famous "Chinese Trinity" of stir-fry tastes—aromatic garlic, ginger, and scallions.

2 lb. assorted mushrooms, such as cremini, portobello, shiitake, enoki, and small yellow or pink oyster mushrooms (but not gray!)

2 tablespoons peanut oil

2 garlic cloves, crushed

1 inch fresh ginger, grated

6 scallions, finely sliced

1 teaspoon sugar

2 teaspoons soy sauce

sprigs of cilantro, Asian mint, or basil, to serve

Serves 4

To prepare all the mushrooms, brush the cremini and portobellos with a soft cloth and trim the ends off the stalks. Slice in half lengthwise. Remove the stems from the shiitakes and cut the caps in half. Slice the end of the roots off the enokis. Leave the oyster mushrooms whole.

Heat the oil in a wok. Add the garlic, ginger, and scallions and stir-fry for about 20 seconds, then add the firmer kinds of mushrooms. Stir-fry for a few minutes, add the sugar and soy sauce, and stir-fry quickly until the sugar is dissolved. Add the oyster mushrooms and enokis, turning gently in the sauce without breaking them up. Transfer to a serving plate, sprinkle over the herbs and serve with rice or meat dishes.

vegetables

zucchini and beans
in spicy coconut milk

This simple dish of Southeast Asian flavors is one of my favorite ways to serve vegetables—spicy, barely cooked, but bathed in coconut milk. I have used pretty little pattypan squash, sugarsnap peas, and Chinese long beans, which keep their crunch and bite better than ordinary beans, but you should use whichever crisp vegetables are in season and freshest at the market.

Put the pattypan squash, zucchini, and Chinese long beans in a steamer and cook over simmering water until *al dente* (about 3 minutes). Add the sugarsnaps, wing beans (if using), tomatoes, and asparagus tips and steam for about 1–2 minutes more until heated through.

Put the coconut milk, fish sauce, sugar, and chili flakes (if using) in a wok or saucepan and heat, stirring, to boiling point—coconut milk must be stirred as it heats, or it will curdle; similarly, it should never be covered with a lid.

Add all the vegetables, stir gently, then transfer to a heated serving bowl. Sprinkle with sprigs of cilantro, the sliced chili, and scallions, and serve with other Asian dishes and fragrant Thai rice.

2 cups coconut milk

1 tablespoon fish sauce, such as *nam pla*

1 tablespoon sugar

1 teaspoon dried chili flakes (optional)

your choice of:

4 oz. yellow and green pattypan
   squash, halved

8 yellow or green mini zucchini,
   halved lengthwise

10 Chinese long beans, cut into
   2-inch lengths

8 oz. sugar snap peas

4 oz. wing beans (from Thai, Vietnamese,
   or Chinese shops), (optional)

8 red or yellow cherry tomatoes, halved

12 asparagus tips (optional)

to serve

8 sprigs of cilantro

1 fresh red chili, sliced

2 scallions, sliced

Serves 4

stir-fried water chestnuts and sprouts

3 tablespoons peanut or safflower oil

2 garlic cloves, crushed

1 lb. baby Brussels sprouts, trimmed
and halved

1 lb. canned water chestnuts, drained
and sliced

¼ cup rice wine, ginger wine, or dry sherry

a pinch of salt

Serves 4

This is a Chinese-inspired variation on the French dish of sprouts and sweet chestnuts. Cabbagey things like sprouts should not be cooked longer than a few minutes, or they stink! This is the perfect solution to the problem.

Heat the oil in a wok, add the garlic, and stir-fry quickly until golden. Add the sprouts and water chestnuts and stir-fry for a few seconds. Add the rice wine, salt, and ½ cup water. Cover the wok, reduce the heat, and steam for about 1–2 minutes, or until the sprouts are lightly cooked but not soft.
Serve immediately with other dishes as part of a Chinese meal, or as an accompaniment to meat or poultry cooked in the Western style.

vietnamese stir-fried bok choy

2 tablespoons peanut or safflower oil

1 garlic clove, crushed

1 inch fresh ginger, grated

3 stalks lemongrass, finely sliced

2 scallions, chopped

2 red chilies, finely sliced

1 tablespoon fish sauce, such as *nuóc mam*

1 tablespoon sugar

2 lb. baby bok choy, halved lengthwise

2 tablespoons Chinese rice wine

Serves 4

Stir-frying is the perfect way to preserve the taste, color, and nutrients of good fresh vegetables—and Asian cooks are past masters at the art.

Heat the oil in a wok, add the garlic, ginger, lemongrass, scallions, chilies, fish sauce, and sugar, and stir-fry for 1–2 minutes.
Add the bok choy and 1 tablespoon water and stir-fry for 1 minute until lightly wilted. Sprinkle with the rice wine, stir once, and serve.

vietnamese pancakes
with bean sprouts and scallions

The Vietnamese branch of my family usually fills these pancakes with shrimp, shredded duck, or stir-fried pork strips, as well as the vegetables, and you could too. However, finding myself shrimpless one day, I tried this vegetarian version, and I love it!

To make the pancakes, mix the two flours, turmeric, sugar, and scallions in a bowl. Mix the coconut milk, eggs, and fish sauce in a small pitcher, then gradually stir into the flour mixture to form a smooth batter. Set aside.

Heat 1 tablespoon of the oil in a wok, add the onions, if using, and stir-fry until soft and golden. Remove from the wok with a slotted spoon and reserve.

Add 1 teaspoon oil to the wok, swirl around to coat the surface, and heat well. Pour a quarter of the batter into the wok and swirl it around to cover the surface thinly. Put a quarter of the mushrooms, bean sprouts, chili, and onions (if using) in the middle of the pancake. Cover with a lid, turn the heat to the lowest possible, and cook for about 3 minutes or until the filling is heated through. Using a spatula, fold the pancake in half like a French omelet, transfer to a serving plate, and keep it hot. Repeat until you have 4 pancakes.

Serve immediately with a separate plate of lettuce leaves, mint or basil, and cilantro, if using. Each person puts a piece of the pancake in a lettuce leaf, adds sprigs of mint, basil, or cilantro, rolls up the leaf, and eats it either plain or dipped into *nuớc cham* or chili dipping sauce.

4 onions, finely sliced (optional)
20 shiitake mushrooms, stems removed and discarded, caps sliced
1 small package bean sprouts, trimmed
1 red chili, finely sliced (optional)
corn or peanut oil, for frying

coconut pancakes

½ cup rice flour
¼ cup cornstarch
1 teaspoon ground turmeric
1 teaspoon sugar
8 scallions (white and green), sliced diagonally crosswise
¼ cup coconut milk
2 eggs, beaten
1 tablespoon fish sauce, such as *nuớc mam*

to serve

lettuce leaves
sprigs of Asian mint or basil
cilantro sprigs (optional)
nuớc cham (page 11) or chili dipping sauce (page 28)

Serves 4

indonesian
gado-gado salad

2 mini cucumbers, such as Lebanese,
   halved lengthwise and seeded

8 Chinese long beans, cut into
   2-inch lengths

1 orange bell pepper

1 small package bean sprouts, trimmed

2 heads baby romaine lettuce (Little Gem)

7 inches white daikon radish (mooli),
   peeled and grated

1 package shrimp crackers

2 onions, finely sliced into rings

sea salt flakes

peanut oil, for frying

peanut sauce

8 oz. roasted peanuts

1 teaspoon corn or peanut oil

1 garlic clove, crushed

2 red chilies, cored and chopped

1 onion, finely diced

1 tablespoon brown sugar

1 teaspoon lime juice

a pinch of salt

1 cup coconut milk

Serves 4

You can alter the vegetable components of this salad according to what's in season. I like long beans rather than ordinary beans for salads, because they keep their crunch better. This traditional salad can be brought more up-to-date by using the latest fashionable vegetables.

Finely slice the halved cucumbers diagonally, put on a plate, sprinkle with salt, let stand for 10 minutes, then rinse and pat dry with paper towels. Chill.

Cook the Chinese long beans in boiling salted water until *al dente*, then drain, plunge into cold water then cool completely over ice. Pat dry.

Peel the bell pepper with a vegetable peeler, core, and finely slice.

To cook the shrimp crackers, fill a wok one-third full with peanut oil and heat to 375°F. Drop in a piece of noodle to test the temperature—it should fluff up immediately. Add the crackers, crowding them so they curl up, then cook until puffed and golden. Remove and drain on paper towels.

To cook the onion rings, reheat the oil, add the sliced onion, and deep-fry until crisp and golden. Remove and drain on paper towels.

To make the sauce, put the peanuts in a blender or food processor and grind to a coarse meal. Heat the corn or peanut oil in a wok, add the garlic, chilies, and onions and stir-fry until golden. Add the peanuts, sugar, lime juice, salt, and coconut milk and cook, stirring, until thickened.

Arrange the vegetables on serving plates and serve with onion rings, shrimp crackers, and peanut sauce.

index

conversion charts

Weights and measures have been rounded up or down slightly to make measuring easier.

Volume equivalents:

American	Metric	Imperial
1 teaspoon	5 ml	
1 tablespoon	15 ml	
¼ cup	60 ml	2 fl.oz.
⅓ cup	75 ml	2½ fl.oz.
½ cup	125 ml	4 fl.oz.
⅔ cup	150 ml	5 fl.oz. (¼ pint)
¾ cup	175 ml	6 fl.oz.
1 cup	250 ml	8 fl.oz.

Weight equivalents: Measurements:

Imperial	Metric	Inches	Cm
1 oz.	25 g	¼ inch	5 mm
2 oz.	50 g	½ inch	1 cm
3 oz.	75 g	¾ inch	1.5 cm
4 oz.	125 g	1 inch	2.5 cm
5 oz.	150 g	2 inches	5 cm
6 oz.	175 g	3 inches	7 cm
7 oz.	200 g	4 inches	10 cm
8 oz. (½ lb.)	250 g	5 inches	12 cm
9 oz.	275 g	6 inches	15 cm
10 oz.	300 g	7 inches	18 cm
11 oz.	325 g	8 inches	20 cm
12 oz.	375 g	9 inches	23 cm
13 oz.	400 g	10 inches	25 cm
14 oz.	425 g	11 inches	28 cm
15 oz.	475 g	12 inches	30 cm
16 oz. (1 lb.)	500 g		
2 1b.	1 kg		

Oven temperatures:

110°C	(225°F)	Gas ¼
120°C	(250°F)	Gas ½
140°C	(275°F)	Gas 1
150°C	(300°F)	Gas 2
160°C	(325°F)	Gas 3
180°C	(350°F)	Gas 4
190°C	(375°F)	Gas 5
200°C	(400°F)	Gas 6
220°C	(425°F)	Gas 7
230°C	(450°F)	Gas 8
240°C	(475°F)	Gas 9